The authors' thanks to Sidney Waugh, sculptor and designer of fine glass, for his helpful suggestions regarding the manuscript of this book.

FIRST PRINTING

Printed in the United States of America
by The Polygraphic Company of America

Published in Canada by Ambassador Books, Ltd., Toronto 1, Canada

Library of Congress Catalog Nunber: 55-5405

THE FIRST BOOK OF
G·L·A·S·S

by SAM and BERYL EPSTEIN and

Pictures by BETTE DAVIS Williams

FRANKLIN WATTS, Inc.
699 Madison Ave., New York 21

j666.1
Ep88

TOOLS GLASSMAKERS USE

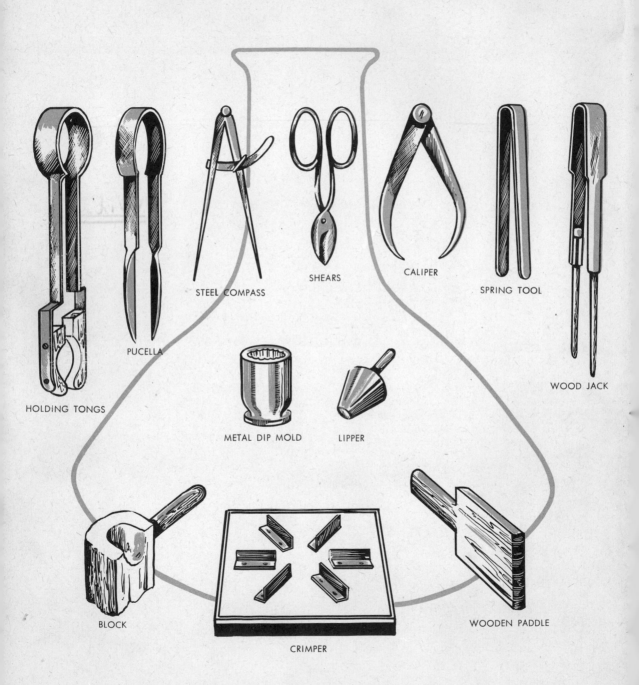

HOLDING TONGS

PUCELLA

STEEL COMPASS

SHEARS

CALIPER

SPRING TOOL

WOOD JACK

METAL DIP MOLD

LIPPER

BLOCK

CRIMPER

WOODEN PADDLE

PONTIL OR PUNTY ROD

BLOWPIPE

Six riddles and one more

What can be as hard as stone or as soft as cotton batting?

What can be as fragile as an egg shell or as strong as steel?

What can let light through or keep light out?

What can be colorless, or colored with all the shades of the rainbow?

What can be almost as light as a feather, or almost as heavy as lead?

What can be as unyielding as concrete, or as flexible as silk?

The answer to each of these riddles is one word: GLASS.

But *how* can any substance be both hard and soft, fragile and strong, transparent and opaque, colorless and many-colored, light and heavy, unyielding and flexible?

The one real answer to this riddle is the whole exciting story behind the remarkable material we call glass.

3

Wood jack and revolving pontil rod were used by this French glassmaker in 1750

Many centuries ago there was just one kind of glass, and people used it only because they admired its beauty. It was hard but fragile. It was greenish in color, and not transparent. It was not very heavy. It was flexible only when it was melted in a high heat. Because the earliest glassmakers did not know how to blow glass, they molded it instead, while it was hot and soft, into glass beads and tiny jars and bottles. And the glass they made was so rare and expensive that only kings and very wealthy men could afford it.

Today glass is everywhere

Today glass is one of the commonest substances in our modern world. We can all afford it. We use it in so many ways that no one can imagine getting along with out it.

We look through glass windows. We drink out of glasses. We buy food in glass containers and cook in glass dishes. We look in a glass to see ourselves, read by the light of a glass bulb, and wear eyeglasses.

Some of us live or work or go to school in buildings that have walls made of glass brick, that are perhaps hung with curtains made of fine-spun glass threads. Glass protects the headlights of our cars, trucks, trains and planes.

Our doctors could not keep us well, or cure us when we are sick, without glass thermometers and hypodermic needles and X-ray tubes. Our scientists could not make new discoveries or invent new things without the glass equipment in their laboratories and the glass lenses of their microscopes and telescopes. Photographers use glass lenses in their cameras. Radio and television sets operate with glass tubes. Movies could not be made or shown without glass.

Many factories and industrial plants must have glass pipes, glass tanks and other apparatus made of glass. Glass objects called insulators protect men and machines and equipment from the dangers of electric current and heat and cold and dampness. Tiny glass fibers strengthen the plastic material that makes safety helmets, luggage, furniture, toys, boat hulls, car bodies and airplane parts.

SOME VERY IMPORTANT USES OF GLASS

Thermometers for doctors, scientists and manufacturers
are made of glass

Glass apparatus in scientific laboratories holds acids
safely, is easily sterilized, and lets scientists watch the
progress of their experiments

X-ray tubes used in medical and research laboratories
are made of glass that permits the passage of the invis-
ible rays we call X-rays

Fruits and vegetables are often preserved in glass jars

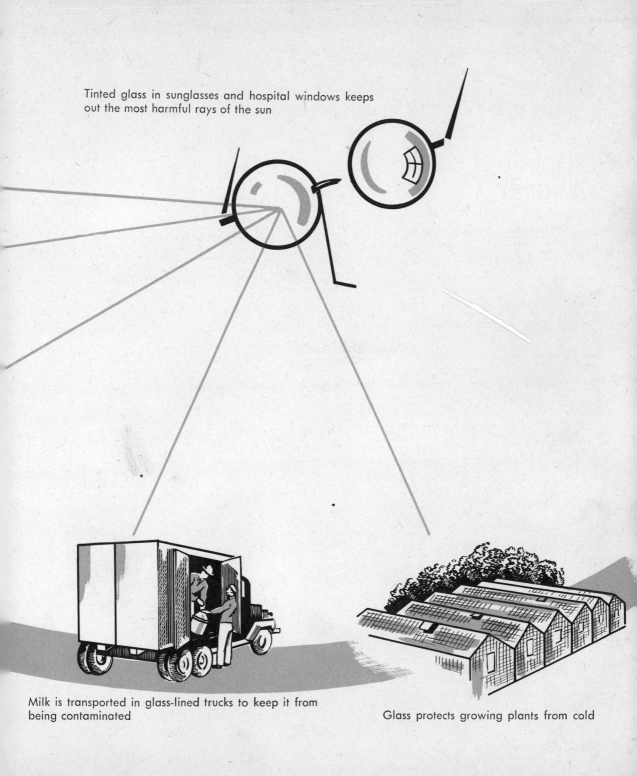

Tinted glass in sunglasses and hospital windows keeps out the most harmful rays of the sun

Milk is transported in glass-lined trucks to keep it from being contaminated

Glass protects growing plants from cold

Today there is no longer just one kind of glass. There are thousands of kinds. And each special kind of glass is made according to a special recipe, or formula, perfected only after years of work by scientists all over the world.

But these scientists are only one of the many groups of people who have played a part in the exciting history of glass — a history which probably began in Asia nearly 10,000 years ago. Nobody is sure who the first glassmakers were, or where and when they lived. We know only that glass is one of the oldest man-made substances in the world.

How to make glass

We make glass today by almost the same basic method that people used thousands of years ago. Here is an ancient recipe for glass:

Take a quantity of fine white sand. Mix with it a little of the chemical called calcium oxide, or lime, and a little of the chemical called sodium carbonate, or soda. Heat this mixture in a furnace until it fuses, or melts. Dip the rod into this molten glass and lift out a gob of it. While it is still soft and hot, mold it into what-

Glass furnace

8

ever shape you wish. Then let the finished object cool and harden.

The chief ingredient of glass is silica. Silica is just another name for fine white sand. Each grain of this sand is a tiny piece of mineral called quartz crystal. Most ordinary sand is a mixture of quartz crystal grains and grains of other minerals. It makes a very poor glass with a greenish color. Most ancient glass was greenish or dark colored because the glassmakers of that time used silica that had bits of iron or other impurities in it.

Silica beds

It is possible to remove all the impurities from ordinary sand, but glassmakers would rather start with sand that is naturally pure, or almost pure silica. For this reason many glass factories are built near the beds of silica in New York, New Jersey, Pennsylvania, Ohio, Illinois and Missouri.

Sometimes glassmakers still add soda to their silica because soda makes the silica melt faster. And sometimes they add bits of old broken glass to the sand and soda. The broken glass melts quickly and turns into a liquid which also makes the silica melt faster. The broken glass is called cullet, and glass factories always have great piles of cullet on hand ready for use.

Sometimes lime is still used too, for certain kinds of glass, but not all modern glass recipes call for it.

9

Each variety of modern glass is made by adding certain special ingredients to the glass mixture, or batch. Gold added to the batch, for instance, gives glass a red color. Lead, together with other things, is added to silica to make very clear, transparent glass. Other substances added to silica make glass that can withstand heat, and glass for other special purposes.

Silica does not melt or fuse until it reaches a temperature of 2,600 degrees. This is nearly eight times hotter than the temperature needed to bake a cake. Some kinds of glass need an even higher temperature, so a glass-furnace fire must be steady and very hot. Glassmakers first used wood as a fuel for their furnaces. Later, they changed to coal, and still later, to gas. Many glass furnaces today are heated by gas or oil.

The container in which a batch of glass is cooked must be made of a fire-resistant clay that will not crack or melt at a high temperature. Sometimes a whole glass furnace is lined with this clay, and then the entire furnace can be used as a huge pot for a big batch of glass. Sometimes this clay is shaped into a small pot, or crucible, for small batches of glass.

If finished glass is allowed to cool quickly, it will be brittle and will break easily. So glassmakers cool it in a lehr, which is a sort of oven. They heat the lehr before they put the glass into it, then cool it very slowly so that the glass inside it cools slowly too. This cooling process is called annealing, and a lehr is sometimes called an annealing oven.

Nature makes glass, too

Whenever silica is heated to a high temperature, it melts and becomes glass. The heat of an erupting volcano can fuse silica and transform it into glass. If lightning strikes down into sand it can form long sticks of glass. If it strikes the surface, it may form a thin glass glaze over the top of the sand. When the atomic bomb was first exploded in the desert of Los Alamos in New Mexico in 1945, the heat of the explosion turned the top layer of sand into a thin glass glaze.

There are many kinds of natural glass, because silica is usually mixed with other substances. Each mixture produces a different kind of glass when it is melted. Here are a few examples of natural glass: obsidian, jasper, rock crystal, quartz, amethyst, agate, onyx.

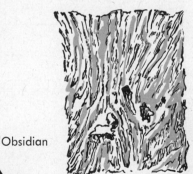

Obsidian

Quartz

Rock crystal, amethyst, agate, onyx and jasper are all forms of quartz

11

Hand-molded glass

Egyptians were the best glassmakers in the ancient world. Even 3,500 years ago they had learned how to make glass in many lovely colors. One beautiful shade of blue glass was invented by an Egyptian king who admired glass so much that he learned how to make it himself.

But the early Egyptian glassmakers did not know how to blow glass. They molded it while it was still hot and soft like putty. They made little glass statues of men and animals, and all sorts of beads and ornaments. They also wrapped threads of hot soft glass around a little core-like shape of hard sand, heated the glass again so that the threads ran together, and then dug out the sand so that they had a hollow glass bottle or jar.

Molding glass was slow, difficult work. A glass bead sometimes cost as much as a rare jewel, and Egyptian queens had bits of glass set into their elaborate gold necklaces. Only queens and wealthy women could afford the little bottles made of glass threads. They carried precious perfumes or cosmetics in them, or hung them from their sashes as ornaments.

A few artists still mold glass by hand today. But hand-molded glass still takes time and skill, and it is still rare and expensive.

12

BOTTLES OLD AND NEW

Cut-glass bottle made in England in the 1700's

Venetian decanter

Medicine bottle, 1900. Bottles were still so expensive that people used the same bottle over and over

A Roman wine jar

Early American bottle

An Egyptian perfume bottle

Modern glass bottle

13

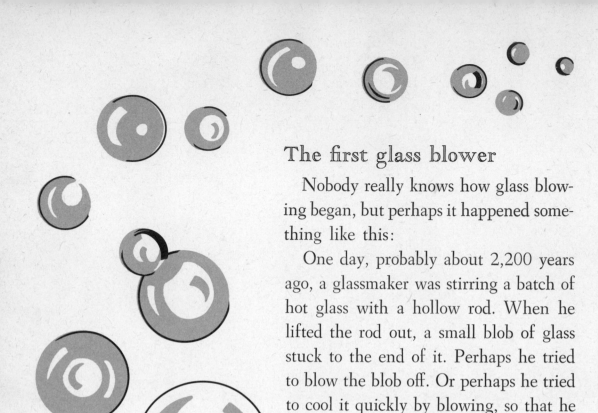

The first glass blower

Nobody really knows how glass blowing began, but perhaps it happened something like this:

One day, probably about 2,200 years ago, a glassmaker was stirring a batch of hot glass with a hollow rod. When he lifted the rod out, a small blob of glass stuck to the end of it. Perhaps he tried to blow the blob off. Or perhaps he tried to cool it quickly by blowing, so that he could break it off. In any case, for some reason he did blow into the other end of his rod.

If you have ever blown soap bubbles you can guess what happened. The liquid glass swelled out into a round hollow bubble. This glassmaker had discovered how to blow glass. He had changed the whole history of glass.

14

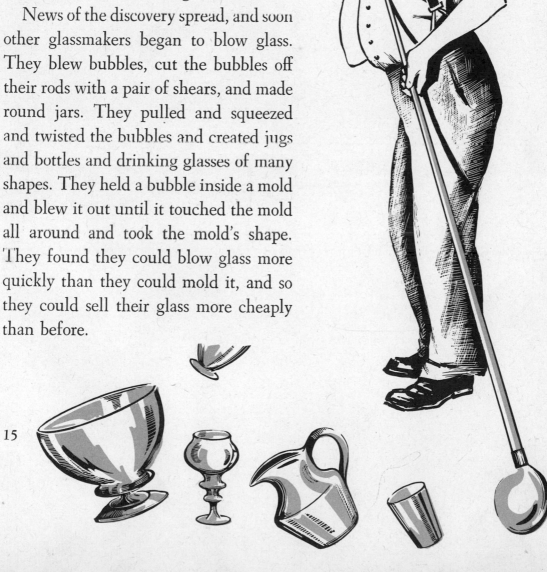

This important event probably took place in Syria, homeland of the Phoenicians, who were famous glassmakers.

News of the discovery spread, and soon other glassmakers began to blow glass. They blew bubbles, cut the bubbles off their rods with a pair of shears, and made round jars. They pulled and squeezed and twisted the bubbles and created jugs and bottles and drinking glasses of many shapes. They held a bubble inside a mold and blew it out until it touched the mold all around and took the mold's shape. They found they could blow glass more quickly than they could mold it, and so they could sell their glass more cheaply than before.

15

ASIA

Glass is useful as well as beautiful

People soon discovered that glass was useful as well as beautiful. They found out that glass jars, for example, were better than clay or wooden jars, for glass doesn't rot away, as wood does. It doesn't wear out. Insects can't eat holes in it, or chew it to pieces. It keeps its shape and color even when it is exposed to the weather for many years. It holds liquids without leaking. It has no taste, and so it can't change the taste of things it holds. Milk kept in a metal jug may taste of the metal, but milk kept in a glass jug will taste of nothing but milk. And glass doesn't absorb the taste or the color

16

EUROPE

or the smell of the liquid that is kept in it. If oil is stored in a glass jar for several months, the jar can be washed out and then used for milk. There will not be any oil taste or color or smell left in the jar to hurt the milk.

When they learned how useful glass is, more and more people wanted to buy it. By the year 100 B.C. glassmakers were very busy, especially in Egypt and Syria and other countries near by. And trading ships carried their wares far across the seas to distant lands.

Glassmaking, which had always been an art, became an important industry in the ancient world.

17

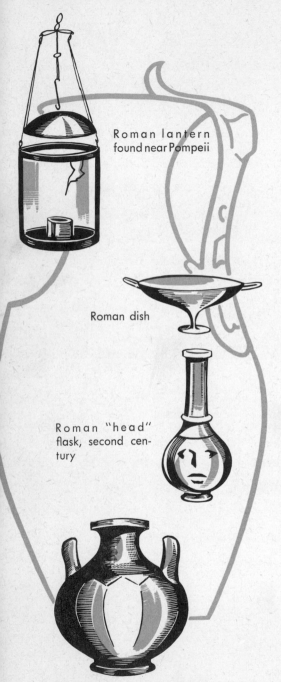

Roman lantern
found near Pompeii

Roman dish

Roman "head"
flask, second cen-
tury

Glass urn to hold ashes of the
dead

The first golden age of glass

In the first century, the center of the new glass industry moved to Rome. Rome had conquered Egypt and Syria and now, because glassmaking had become so profitable, she forced the glassmakers to come to her. The Egyptian and Syrian glassmakers set up their furnaces in Rome and taught glassmaking to Romans.

Rome sent glassmakers all over her vast empire, which stretched south into Africa, east into Asia and north into Europe. But for three hundred years the best glass, and the largest quantities of it, were made in Rome. Those three centuries are known as the first Golden Age of Glass, which means that the finest and most beautiful glass yet known was made at that time.

Roman housewives used glass dishes and containers. Roman merchants used glass storage jars. Chemists used glass bottles. Both men and women wore glass buttons and many kinds of glass orna-

18

ments. When a Roman died, his body was burned and his ashes were put in a glass urn.

Rome used glass in her trade with other lands, and it made her rich and powerful. But when the Roman Empire was finally destroyed by the barbarian tribes from the north, the glass industry was almost destroyed, too. The barbarians were not interested in glass. They thought it was too fragile to be useful.

Across the Mediterranean, a few glassmakers went on with their work. But in the rest of the world, for several hundred years, the art of glassmaking was almost forgotten.

The second golden age of glass

The second Golden Age of Glass, which also lasted some three centuries, began in about the year 1200, in the rich and beautiful city of Venice. Venice started a glass industry just as Rome had done, by bringing glassmakers from across the Mediterranean. She supplied them with fuel from her forests, and good sand from the islands on which the city stood. She encouraged her finest young citizens to study with them.

Soon Venice produced the best glass the world had ever seen. People didn't buy it because it was useful, however, but because it was so beautiful. And they paid such high prices for it that the treasury of Venice overflowed with gold.

19

In certain museums today you can still see examples of the Venetian artists' work. They blew their glass into lovely shapes. Sometimes they painted it with brilliant enamel or shining gold, or made patterns on the surface with threads of hot glass, in the same way that bakers make patterns with colored icing on a cake. Sometimes they modeled a little glass dolphin or dragon or prancing horse, and used it for the handle on a bowl or the stem of a goblet. One kind of decoration which they often used was called millefiori, which means a thousand flowers. A glassmaker held a bunch of colored glass rods in a fire until they melted into a single rod. Then he cut slices from it and melted them onto a glass surface. The melted slices made clusters of tiny colored dots that looked like bouquets of tiny flowers.

The Venetians colored their glass in many beautiful shades of red, blue, green, amber and brown. But their most famous glass had no color at all. The Romans had tried to make colorless glass, but they could never remove all the impurities from their silica, and so their glass always had at least a faint tinge of color. The Venetians were the first to make clear, transparent glass.

Venice jealously guarded her glassmaking secrets from other

20

Venetian glass

countries. She forced all the glassmakers to live and work on one small island which was always protected against spying eyes. If any foreigner tried to sail his gondola close to this island, he was stopped and questioned. And if a Venetian glassmaker tried to leave the city to work somewhere else, or if he tried to give away or sell his secret knowledge, the government's police arrested him as a traitor to Venice.

But even the secret police of Venice could not prevent the knowledge of glassmaking from spreading slowly into other lands. Glasshouses, which means places where glass is made, finally were started in France, Spain, England, Germany, Holland and Bohemia. Usually the king of each country, or a few noblemen, owned or controlled that country's glassmaking, and most of the profits went into the royal treasury.

Some of the new glasshouses invented their own methods of decoration and their own colors. Bohemian glasshouses, for example, made a beautiful new shade of red glass, and cut designs into glass by using fine-ground diamond dust. English glasshouses made glass so beautiful that from 1700 to 1800 England became the center of the glass industry.

21

Bohemian glass   English glass

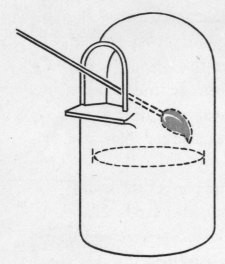

He dips a blowpipe into the metal and lifts up a gob of it

Making hand-blown glass

The modern artist in glass uses the same tools and methods the ancient glass blowers used. He even sits in the same kind of chair. His assistants call him the master, or gaffer. Gaffer is an old English word for grandfather. The assistants watch him very carefully, because they hope to be masters some day too.

Let's say the master has decided to make a pitcher. He has a sketch of it tacked on the wall near his chair. He will use clear, colorless glass. A small furnace of molten glass, which he calls his metal, is in the room where he works.

First his assistant dips a long hollow pipe or rod, called a blowpipe, into the metal and lifts up a gob of it. He rolls the gob back and forth on a flat piece of metal, called a marver, to smooth it out. Then he puts the white-hot glass, still

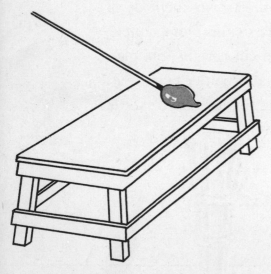

He rolls the gob back and forth on a marver

22

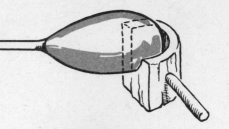

He puts the hot glass into a hollowed-out block of wood

attached to the blowpipe, in a hollowed-out block of wood and turns it around and around until it forms a crude cylinder. Now it is ready for the master.

The master blows gently into the pipe until a small bubble forms inside the gob of metal. The more he blows the larger the bubble grows, and the thinner its wall becomes. Whenever he pauses to rest, he rolls his blowpipe back and forth on the long arms of his chair so that the glass will keep its shape.

To stretch the round ball into a cylinder the length of a pitcher, he lets it sag of its own weight for a moment from the end of his rod. He narrows the pitcher's neck by squeezing the glass with the tool called a jack. If the glass grows cool and stiff, his assistant reheats it in the hole in the side of the furnace called a glory hole.

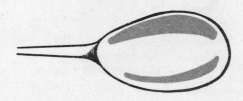

The master blows into the pipe until a bubble forms inside the gob of metal

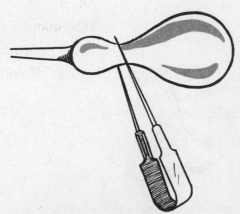

He narrows the pitcher's neck by squeezing the glass with a jack

23

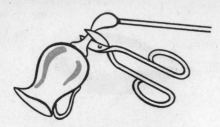

The assistant fuses a bit of hot glass to the bottom of the pitcher

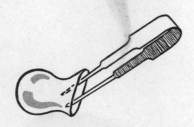

With his jack, the master smooths and flares out the opening to make the lip

He cuts off what he does not need of the ribbon

He attaches the free end to the neck of the pitcher

When the pitcher is finally shaped, the assistant picks up a bit of hot glass on the end of a light rod called a pontil rod, or punty, and fuses it to the pitcher's bottom. Then the master cuts his blowpipe away from the top of the pitcher with a pair of special shears. This leaves a jagged hole for the opening.

Now the master heats the jagged edge of the opening and smoothes it off. He flares it out with his jack to make the lip. Then, working very fast, he takes a fresh gob of hot glass shaped like a thick ribbon and touches one end of it to the pitcher near the bottom. He cuts off what he does not need of the ribbon with his shears, loops the remainder up and attaches the free end to the neck of the pitcher. This is the pitcher's handle.

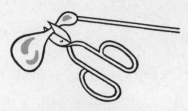

He makes a small bubble from a fresh gob of glass

Next, the master makes a small bubble from a fresh gob of glass, transfers it to a punty and cuts it off his blowpipe. With his punty he widens the hole left by his pipe, flares it back, and then twirls the glass until it flattens into a disc. This will be the pitcher's base, or foot.

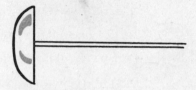

To make the pitcher's base, he widens the hole and flattens it

He removes the pitcher from its punty with a single sharp blow of one of his tools. Then he holds the pitcher by its neck, and with an instrument that looks like a pair of scissors, he fuses the foot to its bottom with a bit of hot glass.

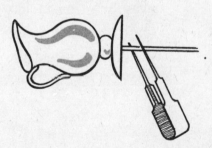

He fuses the foot to the bottom

Finally he removes the punty from the foot with another sharp blow and smooths off the rough spot where the glass broke by heating it for a moment. The pitcher is finished. Now the assistant will take it to the lehr to cool.

With a sharp blow, he removes the punty from the finished pitcher

Cheaper glass

As long as glass was made by hand, it was expensive. And it was expensive just as long as kings could say, "There will be only one glasshouse in my country. All the glass it makes will be sold at a high price, and a share of the profits will belong to me." Sometimes a glass goblet cost more than a goblet made of gold or silver.

But kings finally had to give up some of their rights to the people. More glasshouses started up, and there was competition among them to see who could make glass cheapest and in greatest quantity. Everybody wanted to buy glass, if only the price was low enough.

In 1825 a man named Deming Jarves built a famous glass factory in the village of Sandwich on Cape Cod. He had discovered a faster way of using molds. He poured hot molten glass into the bottom half of a mold and pressed down the upper half with a plunger. Then he opened the mold and removed the finished object.

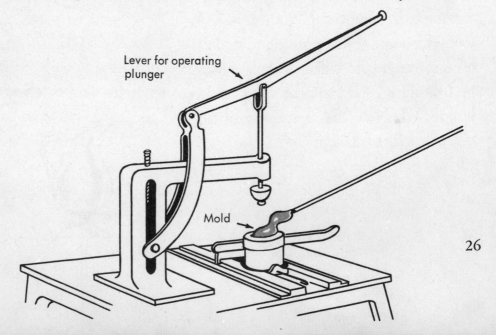

Lever for operating plunger

Mold

26

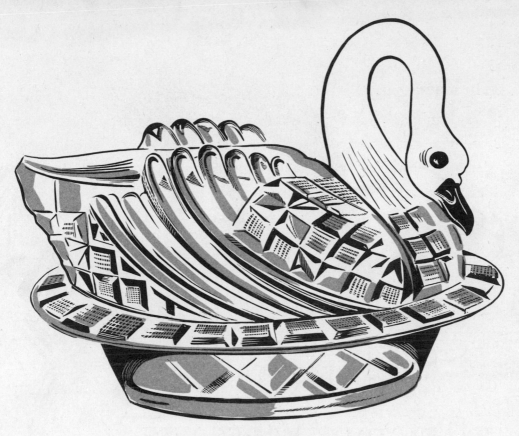

Sandwich glass egg dish

This pressing machine could be used only for dishes or drinking glasses, but it could turn out a hundred drinking glasses in a single hour. Many of the molds were deeply carved, so that Sandwich glass looked as if it had designs cut into it, like the expensive hand-cut glass that English glasshouses were making at that time. Deming Jarves could sell his glass so cheaply that thousands of Americans could buy it. Five hundred men and boys worked in his big factory. It was the first really large-scale glass factory in the world.

And finally, in 1903, another man named Michael Owens invented the first glass-blowing machine. It had fifteen long arms like the spokes of a wheel. There was a bottle-shaped mold at the end of each spoke. As the machine revolved, each arm picked up a blob of molten glass and blew it into the mold by means of compressed air. Then the mold automatically opened and set the bottle down on a moving belt that carried it to the lehr.

Michael Owens' glass-blowing machine turned out hundreds of bottles in a very few minutes. They were not as beautiful as the bottles blown by skillful Venetian artists, and they were all alike. But they were the beginning of glass as we know it now — glass so plentiful that everybody can afford to use it every day, in all sorts of ways.

Many factories soon began to use bottle-blowing machines, and millions of glass bottles began to flood the world. Similar machines also produced drinking glasses and other kinds of blown glass. Owens' invention was the most important event in the history of glassmaking since the blowing of the first glass bubble thousands of years ago.

GLASSHOUSES OF YESTERDAY

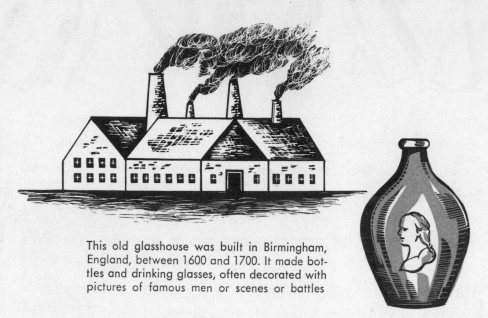

This old glasshouse was built in Birmingham, England, between 1600 and 1700. It made bottles and drinking glasses, often decorated with pictures of famous men or scenes or battles

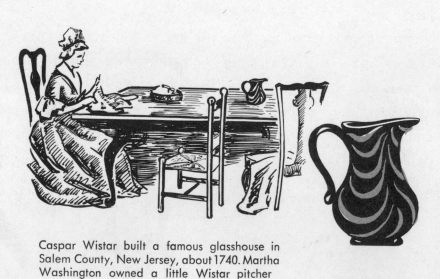

Caspar Wistar built a famous glasshouse in Salem County, New Jersey, about 1740. Martha Washington owned a little Wistar pitcher

A few years before the American Revolution, William Henry Stiegel built a glasshouse in Mannheim, Pennsylvania. He hired a hundred glassmakers from Europe, and each one made the kind of glass he knew best. People called Stiegel the "Baron" because he lived as grandly as a nobleman

Captain John Smith built this small glasshouse at Jamestown, Virginia, soon after the settlement of the first English colony in America

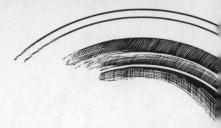

Inlaying the glass mosaic of an angel on the wall of the Hagia Sophia

Detail of a glass mosaic from the Hagia Sophia

Pictures made with glass

In the ancient city of Istanbul, once called Constantinople, there stands a building whose walls are covered with remarkable pictures made of glass. The building is called the Hagia Sophia, which means Divine Wisdom. It was the mother church of the early Christians, and it was built nearly 1,500 years ago. The pictures were made at that time, and most of them are portraits of Christian saints.

These pictures, called glass mosaics, were made by setting small pieces of colored glass into the fresh plaster of the church's walls and vast domed ceilings. When the plaster hardened, the pieces of glass were firmly fixed in place.

32

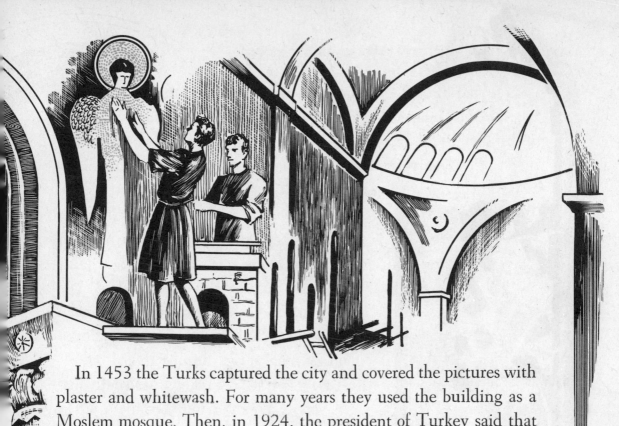

In 1453 the Turks captured the city and covered the pictures with plaster and whitewash. For many years they used the building as a Moslem mosque. Then, in 1924, the president of Turkey said that the Hagia Sophia should become a museum. Men chipped away the whitewash and plaster, and now the pictures are visible again.

Glass mosaics were not new, even when these pictures were made. More than 2,000 years ago the ancient Greeks imported glass from Egypt so that they could make glass mosaics on the walls and floors of their houses. Today artists make glass mosaics, too. On one wall of a building at Rockefeller Center, in New York, there is a big picture made of tiny pieces of glass set into plaster. But the mosaics in the Hagia Sophia, with backgrounds made of thousands of dazzling gold-covered cubes, are probably the finest ever made.

A second kind of glass decoration, also used in this church, was much newer and more surprising when the church was built. The openings of the church's carved stone windows were filled with small pieces of colored glass that transformed rays of sunshine into shafts of beautiful rainbow-colored light.

A few centuries later, when Christian monks and priests went north from Constantinople into Europe, they built churches that also had bits of colored glass in their windows. The monks had to make their own glass because there were almost no glassmakers in Europe then.

At that time a window was usually just an empty hole cut into a wall to let in light. Of course the opening let in the cold, too, and the wind and the rain. Sometimes people covered their windows with pieces of cloth or animal skins. This kept out some of the cold, but it kept out most of the light, too. The colored or stained glass windows kept out the cold and let in the light.

These stained glass windows were useful in still another way. The early priests had no paintings or drawings. But the

34

Stained glass window

bits of colored glass in their windows, fitted together with thin lead strips, could take the form of pictures of Christ and His apostles, and could illustrate religious parables. These pictures helped people to understand the Bible stories the priests told them.

Some of the colored windows those monks made can still be seen today. Many people go to see them every year, to admire their rich, deep colors and their beautiful designs.

The bits of glass in the windows of the Hagia Sophia, and the colored glass windows in the old churches of Europe, were the ancestors of all the glass windows of our modern world. But here is a strange fact: the men who made those wonderful colored windows could not make a single pane of clear, smooth window glass of the kind that is so common today. Even the Venetians, who discovered how to make clear, transparent glass, couldn't make an ordinary windowpane because they didn't know how to make a sheet of smooth, flat glass big enough to fill an ordinary modern window.

Modern picture window

Bull's eye plate

Learning to make modern window glass

Many centuries went by before people learned to make flat glass. The earliest method was called the crown method. Glassmakers pricked open a glass bubble and widened the hole by pulling the soft glass back until the bubble looked like a half-open flower. Then they twirled the bubble around until it flared out into a flat disc. It was the same method they used when they made the flat foot of a bowl or a goblet.

At the center of the disc, where it had been attached to the rod, there was always a thick, fat lump of glass left. This was sometimes called the bull's eye, but usually it was called the crown, and that's why this kind of glass was called crown glass. This thick central piece of glass was almost useless for windows, because very little light could get through it.

The edges of the disc, cut into pieces, were the only kind of window glass known for many hundreds of years. The pieces were always small, because the disc itself was not very large. People had to fit many of these pieces together with strips of wood or lead to fill a window. American colonists made all their windows in this way.

A much better method than the crown method for making flat glass was invented about eight hundred years ago, but for seven hundred years few men used it because it required a great deal of time and skill. It was called the cylinder method, and it began with a bubble, just as the crown method did. The glassmaker allowed this bubble to hang down from his twirling rod until it sagged out into a cylinder. Then he opened the end of the cylinder and cracked the cylinder off the rod. Next he split it from top to bottom with the point of a diamond, and laid it on a table and reheated it. It opened out a little as it softened with the heat, and men flattened it down on the table with tools that looked like wooden hoes.

The outer surface of the cylinder was always a little larger than the inner surface, and it bulged into wrinkles as they worked. The wrinkles gave the glass a wavy appearance, and everything on the other side of it also looked wavy, or distorted.

In 1903, a man who worked as a glass-flattener invented a machine for blowing cylinders 30 inches in diameter and 40 feet long. The glassmaker who operated this machine had to ride upward on an elevator as the cylinder lengthened out. This machine made window glass much cheaper and more common than it had ever been before, but it was still wavy and uneven.

American small-paned window, built in 1666

This American colonial house, built about 1600, has only one window. Glass was so expensive that few people could afford glass windows. Some governments taxed them as luxuries

The front wall of the General Assembly Building of the United Nations, in New York, is made of glass that has been treated to look like marble

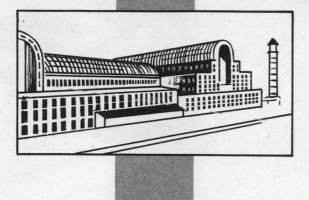

This is the Crystal Palace, designed by an English gardener, and built in London for the Great Exhibition of 1851. It was made of 300,000 sheets of cylinder glass, each 49 inches long and 10 inches wide

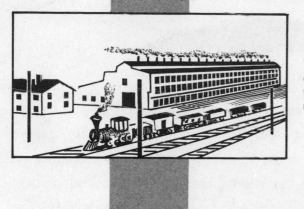

This many-windowed building is a factory, built about 150 years ago. Early factories had more windows than private houses because workers needed light to operate their machines

This modern bank, on Fifth Avenue in New York, has walls of glass

Plate glass

Although we think of plate glass as one of our modern inventions, it was actually invented in 1668 by a French glassmaker named Louis Lucas. Lucas poured hot molten glass onto a sand-covered table and rolled it out with big rollers, as if he were making a sheet of glass pie crust. Long ago, in the first Golden Age of Glass, Roman glassmakers had tried to make flat glass in this way, but they were not successful. But Lucas, by grinding off the sandy surface, produced a sheet of fine, clear glass. It was bigger than the pieces of glass made by the crown method, and it wasn't wrinkled like cylinder glass. He called it plate glass, because he made it in a flat plate, or sheet. For several centuries nobody even thought of using it for windows. They used it only for very expensive mirrors.

Finally, during World War I, a method was invented for making sheets of flat glass by machine. Each sheet was pulled or forced out of a great tank of molten glass and carried away between rollers. Several of these sheet-making machines were invented about the same time. One of them made an endless ribbon of glass, four feet wide, that ran from the furnace through the annealing oven to the shipping room, where it was cut into squares and packed in boxes. It produced 30,000 square feet of glass every twenty-four hours.

Plate glass, which is heavier and thicker than ordinary window glass, is now also produced by machine. When the ribbon of glass comes out of the annealing oven, it travels through huge automatic grinding machines that smooth its surface as it moves steadily along, at the rate of about three and a quarter miles a day. It can be cut into pieces of any desired length when it is finished. One of these machines once operated steadily for two years and turned out 1,900 miles of plate glass without stopping.

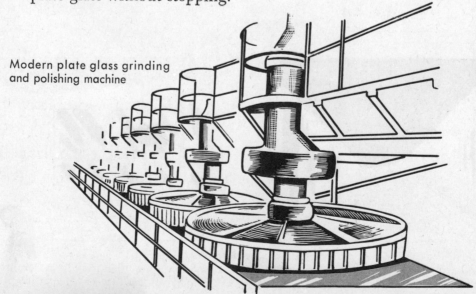

Modern plate glass grinding and polishing machine

BUILDING WITH GLASS

The light that comes through a glass brick wall is diffused, or spread out, to reduce glare and brightness

Houses built in cold regions often have double windows. The air in the space between the panes of glass keeps out the cold, keeps in the warmth

Glass tile lines the roof of the Lincoln Tunnel that runs under the Hudson River from New York to New Jersey

Translucent glass makes walls for hospitals, schools and other buildings. Light shines through it, but it is not clear enough to see through

Windows in cars, trains and planes are made of safety glass, which is two thin layers of glass with a filling of tough plastic, designed to stick together if the glass breaks

Bullet-resistant glass is made like safety glass, but with many layers of glass and plastic

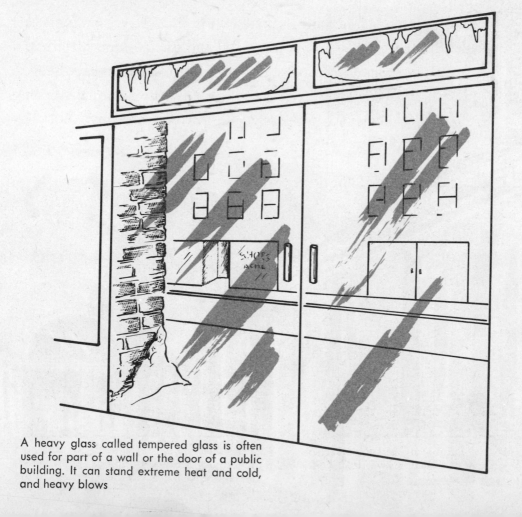

A heavy glass called tempered glass is often used for part of a wall or the door of a public building. It can stand extreme heat and cold, and heavy blows

Glass to see ourselves in

Do you know what you look like? Of course you do, because you can look in a good, clear mirror that shows you exactly as you are.

A modern mirror is any good piece of smooth, flat glass that has been coated on one side with a thin film of silver. When you hold the silvered side away from you, you can see through the glass but not through the metal behind it. The silver catches your image and returns it to you through the glass.

Once people had no mirrors at all except the still, clear waters of a pool. Then they learned to polish metal and use its shiny surface as a mirror. But a metal mirror usually gave blurred or crooked images.

The first good glass mirrors were made by the Venetians during the second Golden Age of Glass. The mirrors were tiny, but they

sold at very high prices. Wealthy ladies wore them dangling from their belts, as ornaments, and noblemen had pins made of them to fasten their hat plumes.

Other countries tried to learn the Venetians' secret of making mirrors, and France finally succeeded. Within a few years France made finer and bigger mirrors than the Venetians ever made, because plate glass was invented at that time.

At first people didn't know what to do with these big new mirrors. But King Louis the Fourteenth of France showed the world that big mirrors could decorate a room, just as small mirrors decorated a man's hat. He used a long row of mirrors to cover one entire wall of the vast hall in his palace at Versailles. And when other people saw this beautiful Hall of Mirrors, they wanted large mirrors for their homes.

Now mirrors are so cheap that almost every house has many mirrors. A man shaves in front of a small round mirror and a woman uses a mirror when she puts on her makeup. A mirror in a dark corner seems to bring light into that part of the room. A wall of mirrors makes a room seem twice as large as it really is. And a small transparent mirror in the door of a house or an apartment lets people see their visitors before they open the door to them. A transparent mirror reflects an image only when you look into it from a fairly light place such as the hall of an apartment. But the metal backing on it is very thin, so if there is not much light inside the house you can see right through the backing as if the mirror were a piece of ordinary glass.

A dentist uses a tiny magnifying mirror when he examines your teeth. The biggest mirror in the world — it is 200 inches across and weighs twenty tons — is part of the world's biggest telescope at the Mount Palomar Observatory in California.

Today we have all sorts of trick mirrors, too. Pink- or gold-tinted mirrors make people look handsome and healthy. Mirrors that make people look distorted are usually part of the fun at a fair or circus.

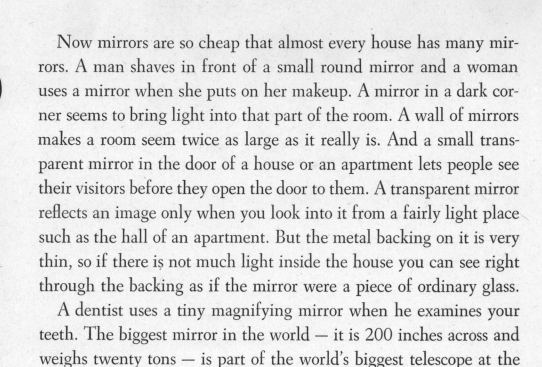

Of course you don't think, as people used to, that the image in your mirror is a spirit who would die if the mirror broke. But haven't you ever wished you could find a

magic mirror world, as Alice did when she stepped through the glass in Lewis Carroll's famous book, *Through the Looking Glass*?

Glass to see with

Some of the people who look at this page are not able to see the words clearly without the help of eyeglasses—a pair of the small round pieces of glass we call lenses. But there is nobody in the whole world who can see clearly a tiny microbe, or a crater on the distant moon, without help.

There are two kinds of lenses. One is shaped something like this ⬭ and is called a magnifying lens. It makes things look larger and closer than they are. The other looks something like this ⋈ and is called a diminishing lens. It makes things look smaller and farther away than they are.

Sometimes an artist looks at his painting through a diminishing lens so that he can see it far away from him, as it will look when it is hung in a big hall or museum. Sometimes the diminishing lens is combined with magnifying lenses to make scientific instruments.

About 350 years ago the Italian scientist Galileo fitted several lenses together inside a long tube to make the first telescope. Through it he saw things in the skies that men had never seen before. People believed, in those days, that the earth stood still and the sun traveled around it. Galileo proved by what he saw through his telescope that the earth travels around the sun. Today we are learning a great deal about the space around the earth and the countless stars in the sky beyond that space, because we can study them in our great modern telescopes.

All the photographs we look at, in books and magazines and newspapers, and on movie and television screens, are possible because the camera was invented. And the camera needs lenses, too.

But there is still one more important way in which we use lenses, and this one is perhaps the most important of all. We uses lenses to make our microscopes.

48

About three centuries ago a Dutch cloth merchant looked at a drop of water under a tiny lens he had made for himself. His name was Anton van Leeuwenhoek, and his lens was the first microscope. With his microscope, in that drop of water, he saw tiny moving creatures which he called little "beasties." He thought them so interesting that he could not destroy a single one. So he made a new microscope every time he wanted to look at a new drop of water. Finally his house was full of microscopes. But he did not know how important his "beasties" were.

It was two hundred years before the great French scientist, Louis Pasteur, discovered that these "beasties," which we call microbes, could turn milk sour and make beer and wine ferment. And he discovered that they could cause disease too.

Today doctors can cure disease and often prevent it entirely because they have learned much about microbes by studying them under powerful microscopes.

Scientists study metals and soils and plants and the human body under microscopes. The things they learn help parents to raise healthier families, farmers to grow better crops, and manufacturers to make better products.

49

How a lens works

To understand how a lens works, we have to know what happens when we see the same thing without a lens. What happens, for example, when you look at the words on this page?

First, the light strikes the page and then bounces away from it, or reflects back from it, toward your eyes. When these light rays reach your eyes they form a tiny image, or picture, of the page on the nerves at the back of your eyes. These nerves send a message about that picture to your brain. When your brain receives the message, you see the words on this page.

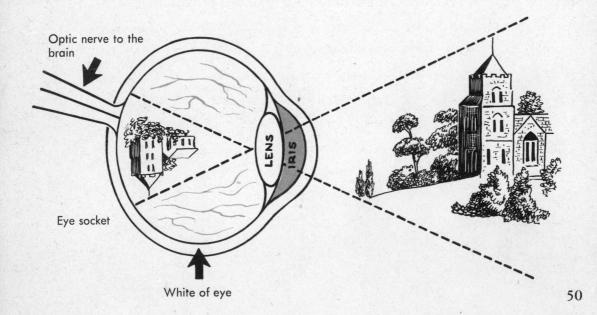

Optic nerve to the brain

LENS

IRIS

Eye socket

White of eye

If you hold a magnifying lens between the page and your eyes, the light rays pass through the lens on the way to your eyes. But they can't go through in a straight line. The curve of the glass makes the rays bend outward, so that they spread like a fan. And the rays carry a big spread-out image to your eyes. When your brain receives this kind of message, you see the words larger than they are. How much larger depends on the power of the lens.

A diminishing lens bends light rays inward, pinches them closer together. You see things smaller than they are.

Only glass that has a curved surface can bend light rays to make us see things larger or smaller than they are. Flat glass lets light rays go straight through. When we look at things through a clear windowpane, we see them the same size they really are.

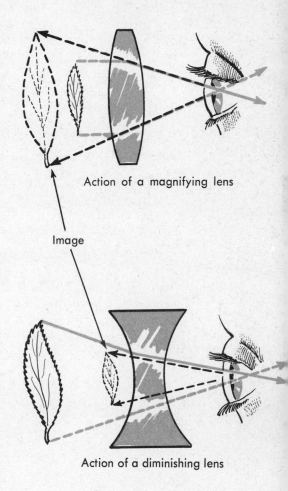

Action of a magnifying lens

Image

Action of a diminishing lens

Shapes of common simple lenses

Sometimes the lenses used in eyeglasses are magnifying lenses. These are worn by people who are farsighted. Without eyeglasses these people can see clearly only those objects which are far away from them. With magnifying eyeglasses, they can see nearby objects too.

Two kinds of magnifying glass, one stronger than the other, are sometimes used in one pair of glasses. These are called bifocal glasses. They were invented by Benjamin Franklin.

Nearsighted people, who have trouble seeing distant objects clearly, are helped by eyeglasses that have diminishing lenses.

The glass for lenses must be very pure. If there is a single air bubble in it, or a tiny grain of unmelted silica, it will not make a good lens. Glass for lenses is called optical glass.

Light inside glass

Did you know that Thomas Edison could never have invented his electric light if he hadn't had a glass globe to put it in? He produced his light by heating a thin wire called a filament with electric current. To keep the filament from burning up, instead of glowing, he had to put it in a vacuum—an enclosed space from which all air has been removed. The wall that enclosed this vacuum had to allow the light to shine through. Glass was the only substance that could form an airtight, transparent wall around this glowing wire.

In 1879, Edison asked a glass factory to make a globe of a certain size and shape. The glass blowers blew 160 bulbs, but none was just right. Then a 15-year-old boy named Fred Deuerlein, assistant to one of the masters, picked up a gob of glass on the end of a blowpipe and blew into it. He blew exactly the kind of globe Thomas Edison wanted!

Older forms of light — candles, kerosene and whale oil lamps and gas lights — were often protected behind glass, too. The glass chimney on a kerosene lamp, for example, shielded the flame from the wind, and yet allowed the light to shine through.

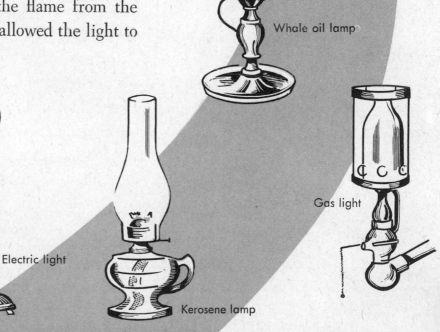

Candle

Whale oil lamp

Gas light

Electric light

Kerosene lamp

Glassmakers have helped many inventors who needed special forms of glass for special kinds of light — for photographers' flash bulbs, for sun lamps, for fluorescent lights and gaily colored neon tubing, and for unbreakable colored signal lights on railroad tracks and automobile highways.

But every day they turn out more and more ordinary electric bulbs to light up cities and farms, hospitals and movie theaters, and all the offices and factories where work goes on around the clock. They also make bulbs so tiny that one can fit on the end of the slender flashlight the doctor puts down your throat to examine your tonsils. The smallest bulb in the world is hardly bigger than a grain of rice. The largest is almost a yard tall.

The largest lamp in the world

Today, in the United States alone, glassmakers produce more than two million light bulbs each year. And certain glass bulb makers, during a few weeks each year, change the molds on their glassblowing machines and make all the glittering ornaments that decorate our Christmas trees.

"Grain of wheat" lamp, the smallest lamp in the world

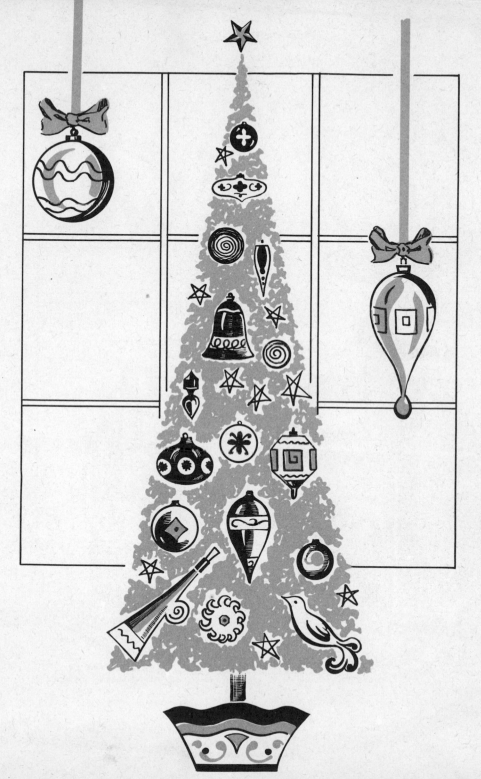

Bottle made to celebrate the opening of the
Erie Canal in 1825

SANDWICH GLASS SLIPPER

THE GODDESS THONERIS
made in Egypt about 330 B.C.

GLASS FOR BEAUTY

GLASS PLATE
designed by Christian Berard for Steuben Glass, Inc.

PERSIAN VASE

GAZELLE BOWL
designed by Sidney Waugh

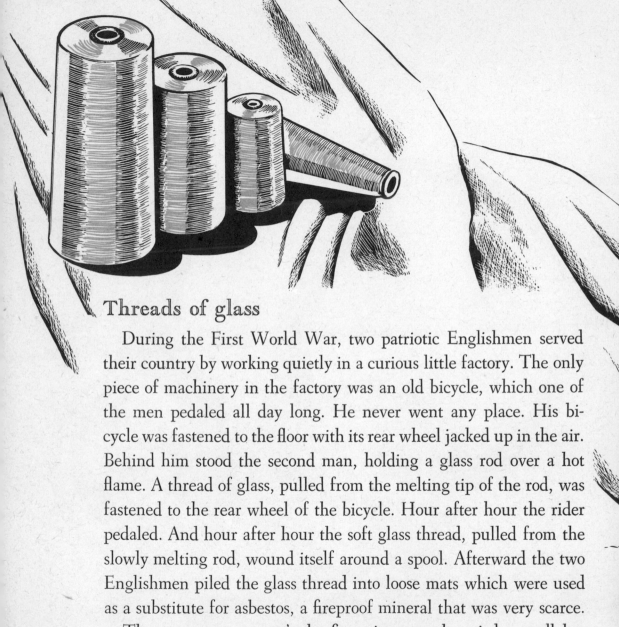

Threads of glass

During the First World War, two patriotic Englishmen served their country by working quietly in a curious little factory. The only piece of machinery in the factory was an old bicycle, which one of the men pedaled all day long. He never went any place. His bicycle was fastened to the floor with its rear wheel jacked up in the air. Behind him stood the second man, holding a glass rod over a hot flame. A thread of glass, pulled from the melting tip of the rod, was fastened to the rear wheel of the bicycle. Hour after hour the rider pedaled. And hour after hour the soft glass thread, pulled from the slowly melting rod, wound itself around a spool. Afterward the two Englishmen piled the glass thread into loose mats which were used as a substitute for asbestos, a fireproof mineral that was very scarce.

These two men weren't the first pioneers who tried to pull hot glass out into strands so thin that they could be bent and twisted and even woven into cloth. And after them still other experimenters worked for many years more, before they finally learned to produce the great quantities of glass threads and fibers the world uses today. Their most difficult problem was to get the threads so thin that they remained flexible even after they cooled. They were sure this could be done, just as they knew it was possible to pull steel out into thin strands of flexible steel wire. But the final solution of the problem came very slowly.

A few of the glassmakers who first tried to make glass threads hoped that some day they could produce a beautiful, shimmering cloth woven of glass. But most of them, like the two Englishmen, had a more practical purpose. They wanted to make glass thread because they knew it would be useful in many different ways. It would have all the basic qualities of a solid piece of glass.

Glass threads are used to reinforce plastic toys and thousands of other plastic articles

We know what some of these qualities are. Glass doesn't absorb moisture. It doesn't burn. Glass is strong, too, much stronger than a steel wire of exactly the same size. Glass also prevents the passage of electricity—it is a good electrical insulator. And a fluffy mat of glass threads can check the passage of heat.

Underground pipes are wrapped with tape woven out of glass fibers. The tape protects them from attack by moisture, insects and microbes.

The red-hot exhaust pipes of an airplane motor might set the plane afire, but fireproof glass fiber wrapping around the pipes keeps the plane and its passengers safe.

Glass fiber insulating blankets

The great strength of glass makes it very useful to the plastics industry. Plastic is a chemical substance which can be molded into almost any shape, and which is very colorful and inexpensive. But plastic is not very strong. So thin threads of glass fiber are often laid in a mold, before the mold is filled with plastic, to give the plastic object strength. Plastic combined with glass threads in this way is called glass-reinforced plastic. It is used for thousands of articles—toys, dishes, safety helmets, luggage, fishing rods, boats, car bodies and airplane parts.

Today the making of glass threads and fibers is a big industry, one of the newest of all the many modern glass industries but already one of the most important. And yet, like glass itself, it had its beginning centuries ago, when ancient artists in glass wound threads around sand to make tiny bottles.

Glassmakers are proud of the age-long history of glass, but they think the future of glass will be even more dramatic than its past. They are still finding new uses for glass every day, and new reasons to admire this remarkable material that serves us so well in so many different ways.

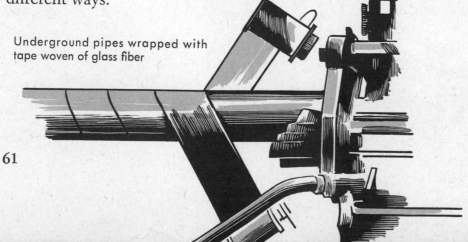

Underground pipes wrapped with tape woven of glass fiber

Did you know that

Scientists have learned many things about the habits of fish by watching them through the floors of glass-bottomed boats?

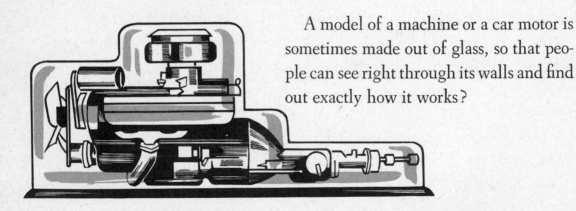

A model of a machine or a car motor is sometimes made out of glass, so that people can see right through its walls and find out exactly how it works?

Delicate flowers like these are sometimes made of glass? Master craftsmen blow them by hand for the use of botany students. Perfect glass copies of fish and microbes and human body cells are also used by science students.

Life-preservers stuffed with glass fibers have saved many lives?

Little glass buttons make road signs that reflect the lights of a car and are easy to see at night?

Expert marble players insist that their shooting marbles be of glass instead of clay, because they shoot straighter?

This curious-looking apparatus can serve as a substitute for a human heart during an operation, when the blood supply to the patient's own heart has to be cut off temporarily?

Words glassmakers use

Annealing oven—same as *Lehr.*

Batch—the mixture of ingredients called for in glassmaking recipes.

Bull's eye—same as Crown.

Crown method—an old method of making window glass by twirling molten glass into discs; the thick blob always left at the center is called a *Crown.*

Crucible—clay container in which glass is made.

Cullet—pieces of old broken glass, added to a new glass batch to hasten fusing.

Cut glass—glass decorated with designs cut into its surface.

Cylinder method—method of making window glass from long glass cylinders; now used chiefly for colored glass windows.

Fuse—to melt ingredients of glass recipe together, in crucible or furnace.

Gaffer—popular term for master glass blower.

Glass blower—craftsman who shapes molten glass by blowing it.

Glass cloth—cloth woven of glass threads.

Glass fibers—tiny shreds of glass that can be piled into mats or spun into thread.

Glass furnace—a furnace in which glass is made.

Glasshouse—a glassmaking factory.

Glass thread—thread made of glass.

Glory hole—small opening in side of glass furnace, for reheating glass while it is being blown or molded.

Hand-blown glass—glass blown by hand, not by machine.

Lehr—oven where freshly made glass objects can be cooled slowly.

Master—a master glass blower.

Metal—glassmakers' name for molten glass.

Mold-blown glass—glass blown into shape inside a mold.

Molten glass—melted, or liquid, glass.

Photo-sensitive glass—glass with a design printed into it by a process somewhat like photography.

Plate glass—thick sheet of glass, finished by grinding to perfect flatness, and highly polished.

Pressed glass—glass made by being pressed into a mold.

Shatter-proof glass—glass which does not shatter when broken; also called *safety glass.*

Silica—Fine white sand.

Tempered glass—special kind of heavy glass which can stand heat, cold and shock.

Translucent glass—any kind of glass which admits light but which is not entirely transparent.

Transparent mirror—mirror with thin backing, transparent from one side.

Index

THE LOBSTER